Cocktails, Mocktails and Smoothies

Cocktails. Mocktails and Smoothies

Published 2013 by arima publishing

www.arimapublishing.com

ISBN 978 1 84549 615 9

A catalogue record of this book is available from the British Library

arima publishing
ASK House, Northgate Avenue
Bury St Edmunds, Suffolk IP32 6BB
t: (+44) 01284 700321

www.arimapublishing.com

Cocktails, Mocktails and Smoothies

Contents

Introduction

Finding the perfect drink to match a particular mood or occasion is never an easy thing. To help with this task First de Sales is proud to present a collection of some of the world's finest cocktail, mocktail and smoothie recipes.

This collection covers a broad range of drinks and includes a mixture of traditional favourites as well as original recipes which are appearing in print for the first time. The entries have been provided by connoisseurs each of whom agreed to contribute their personal favourite cocktail, mocktail or smoothie recipe.

The recipes are easy-to-follow with that extra personal touch that has become the First de Sales trademark. A handy index of ingredients will help you work out which drinks you can make with the contents of even the most meagre drinks cabinet.

Whether you are looking for a relaxing beach drink, a healthy smoothie or a nightclub classic, this book will soon become your indispensable guide to the world of alcoholic and non-alcoholic drinks.

Champagnes
and
Wines

H.E.S.H. (High Explosive: Squash Head)

The regimental drink of a British Army cavalry regiment that shall remain nameless in order to protect the innocent.

A brief history. In the days when the British Army of the Rhine was poised to annihilate the Russian hordes as they swept across what was then West Germany, there was a significant amount of waiting for the attack that we all knew one day would come. The young officers were a long way from their sweet hearts back in England, and were anxious to 'get the party going quickly' whenever there was any chance of female company.

What was required was a long, refreshing and totally innocent tasting but completely lethal cocktail that could be the opening salvo in any skirmish with the opposite sex. The HESH was thus born, named after an anti–armour type of ammunition still used today in anti-tank rounds, so beloved of (for example) the Taliban with the RPG. From my own experience the HESH works every time and, once initiated into the drinking of this fine libation, you tend to take it pretty easy after the first few.

INGREDIENTS
1 part vodka
1 part Cointreau
3 parts champagne
3 parts orange juice

GLASS
Half pint with a handle to stop it warming up quickly in the hand.

GARNISH

None, you don't want to make it too difficult to drink quickly.

STEPS

1 - Place a good handful of ice into a large jug.

2 - Add an appropriate amount of the Cointreau and vodka.

3 - Pour the champagne in carefully as it will effervesce.

4 - Add the orange juice last and serve quickly before the ice melts.

TIPS

The trick to making this delicious drink is that the cocktail is designed to be served around a drinks party or reception in large jugs to enable part-full glasses to be continually refilled. All of the ingredients should be well chilled, including the vodka and Cointreau.

Slogans

A brief history. Sloe gin is a traditional short sharp nip taken in the field during the winter months, and champagne is a treat at any time. A lady accompanying her shooting husband one day couldn't decide which to have and her host suggested that she 'have both at the same time'. The lady's first taste of this new drink resulted in what sounded like a lady at the peak of extreme pleasure, and the cocktail known as 'slogasm' was born to the sound of laughter!

In my own experience, this is a delicious and unusual drink which, like most things in life, is hugely simple to make. The key to it is good sloe gin. I have been lucky enough to have it many times and we restrict it to outside events in winter in order to ensure that it is a truly seasonal drink.

INGREDIENTS

Champagne
Sloe gin

GLASS

Champagne flute

STEPS

1 - Pour about a finger and a half of the sloe gin into the glass.

2 - Top off with champagne. Pour the champagne very slowly so that it does not over flow the glass as this is a waste of champagne and the glass will become very sticky which is a particular problem as the drinker will probably be wearing gloves.

TIPS

Guide to making this delicious drink is that it will be drunk outside on a cold day in winter, so the champagne only needs to be slightly chilled.

Kir Royale

The kir royale is a variant of the kir cocktail, made using champagne rather than white wine. Kir is drunk traditionally as an aperitif and the kir royale as a variant for special occasions.

Kir originates from Burgundy in France. Having been popular in the 19th Century it was given wider appeal and took its name from Canon Félix Kir, a hero of the French Resistance in World War II and the mayor of Dijon until 1968. To encourage local products he mixed together the local white wine made from the Aligoté grape with the local blackcurrant liqueur crème de cassis. The cocktail became hugely popular throughout France and internationally.

INGREDIENTS

4 parts champagne
1 part crème de cassis

GLASS

Champagne flute

GARNISH

None required

STEPS

1 - Pour the crème de cassis into a champagne flute.

2 - Slowly add the champagne.

Lager Royale – A Morning After Drink

A brief history. I am afraid to say that this amazingly simple and refreshing cocktail was born from debauchery. It was invented after a Jeeves and Wooster style weekend of excess. In the books, Jeeves always has a secret hangover concoction, but we never find out what is in it. However, the effects are said to be 'restorative' and enable the party-goer to continue with the merriment of the weekend without any morning ill-effect. The ingredients are usually freely available and plentiful at weekend parties, but are not recommended for drivers. Purists might blanche at the suggestion of adulterating two fine drinks, but needs must when the Devil drives.

I invented this as I was completely unable to touch another drop, having reached the morning of day two of a stag party where I was the organiser and best man. I poured one of these in order to 'see what would happen', and within 10 minutes the whole party was quaffing them. They became a standard morning after drink for all of us, particularly popular at stag parties.

INGREDIENTS
Champagne
Lager (only use a quality brand)

GLASS
Half pint with a handle

GARNISH
Accompany with a bacon and sausage sandwich with a fried egg on top (break the yoke when cooking) and tomato ketchup, with plenty of kitchen roll to hand.

STEPS

1 - Pour just under half a glass of champagne.

2 - Fill up with the lager (this avoids over foaming).

3 - Drink it in mouthfuls, not gulps or sips.

TIP

Guide to making this delicious drink are that the ingredients need to be chilled but not frozen.

The Ruby Dutchess

This elegant champagne-based cocktail was invented at an Easter brunch in a 19th century farmhouse in Rhinebeck, located in Dutchess County, New York. The hostess decided to make the champagne a little more festive by adding some beautiful ruby coloured pomegranate juice and it tasted so delicious we knew it had to have a name!

After a few attempts, the name Ruby Dutchess was suggested, named after the drink's lovely colour and the county it was first discovered in. Its popularity has been growing ever since and has even inspired a range of T-shirts!

INGREDIENTS
4 parts champagne
2 parts pomegranate juice

GLASS
Champagne flute

STEPS
1 - Take one champagne glass, slightly chilled for best results.

2 - Add 50 ml of pomegranate juice.

3 - Pour 100 ml of champagne.

4 - Stir gently and serve!

Moonwalk

Zingy, fresh and fizzy, this tantalising cocktail is allegedly the first drink that Neil Armstrong and Buzz Aldrin sipped upon after their return to Earth in 1969.

INGREDIENTS
Champagne or prosecco to top
30 ml fresh grapefruit juice
30 ml Grand Marnier orange liqueur
2 or 3 drops orange flower water
Ice

GLASS
A chilled champagne flute

GARNISH
1 slice of fresh orange, frozen
1 slice of grapefruit, frozen
Crushed ice

STEPS
1 - Fill a cocktail shaker with ice.

2 - Add grapefruit juice, Grand Marnier and orange water.

3 - Shake vigorously for 10 to 15 seconds.

4 - Strain into a chilled champagne flute and top off with fizz.

5 - Garnish with orange, grapefruit and a handful of crushed ice.

TIP FROM THE BAR
This cocktail is the perfect accompaniment to any breakfast, brunch or lunch as it is light and refreshing and not too overpowering.

Bellini

Giuseppe Cipriani created this seasonal favourite after he opened Harry's Bar in Venice in the 1930s. Named after the famous Venetian painter, it is no longer seasonal, thanks to modern transport and the ready availability of freshly frozen white peach purée.

Once you have the right ingredients, the Bellini can be made easily to serve many guests and is a great cocktail to start a civilised evening, elegant in appearance and flavour, and not too alcoholic. It also makes for a good brunch cocktail, particularly if you over-indulged the night before, and is gentler than orange and fizz.

INGREDIENTS
40 ml white peach purée
120 ml prosecco/sparkling wine

GLASS
Champagne flute

STEPS
1 - Add your 1 part purée to your flute.

2 - Gently add your 3 parts prosecco.

3 - Stir gently.

4 - Serve immediately.

TIP FROM THE BAR
Make sure your ingredients and your glassware are extra cold; almost frozen peach purée works well.

The Pink Lady

Traditionally a girls' gin-based cocktail of the 1930s, this modern alternative Pink Lady recipe has been created with the addition of modern flavoured vodka, in this case that of Black Cherry-flavoured vodka.

The black cherry vodka forms the basis of the Pink Lady. As a result, creating a drink that is refreshing and sweet, appealing to powerful, strong women alike. The addition of Aperol, an Italian aperitif made from bitter orange, balances this drink perfectly, topped as it is with a float of sparkling brut rosé. The Pink Lady is overall a demure cocktail for modern day women, creating a sense of class, sophistication and elegance.

INGREDIENTS
55 ml of black cherry vodka
30 ml of Aperol
Dash of lemon juice
15 ml brut rosé

GLASS
Martini glass

GARNISH
Lemon twist

STEPS
1 - Shake all ingredients together in a cocktail shaker.

2 - Strain into the martini glass.

3 - Top with 15 ml of the Schramsberg (or other) brut rosé.

4 - Garnish with a twist of lemon.

Spanish Sangira

Sangria is served throughout Spain and Portugal during summer and in the southern and eastern parts of the countries year round. In these places it is a popular drink among tourists bars, pubs and restaurants where it is often served in 1 litre pitches or other containers large enough to hold a bottle of wine plus the added ingredients. There are many ways of preparing sangria and almost every Spaniard has his own recipe, here is one of them.

INGREDIENTS

3 peaches
2 oranges
Half a lemon
50 grams of sugar
50 ml of brandy
1 (or a half) litre of red wine
1 branch of cinnamon
1 glass of orange juice
Half a glass of lemon juice
1 spiral lemon peeling

GLASS

Tall glass

STEPS

1 - Peel the peaches, cut them in two and then remove the stone and slice it.

2 - Peel oranges and cut it to pieces.

3 - Put the fruits in a container with the sugar and the brandy and let them soak for about 12 minutes.

4 - Once soaked add the fruit into wine with the two glasses of juice

(orange and lemon).

5 - Add the cinnamon and the spiral lemon peeling and let cool down in the refrigerator.

TIP FROM THE BAR
This drink has to be served very cold. Before serving the sangria, at the last moment add ice cubes or you can add a little bottle of very cold lemonade or orangeade.

Jul Glogg

An excellent drink for outside in the winter. Bonfire night with a piece of parkin or New Year's Eve with a mince pie or even a slice of stollen and fireworks are not the same without the warming glow provided by this fine Scandinavian beverage.

INGREDIENTS

Spices. A bag to include: half a slice of finely chopped lemon or orange peel; 8 ml cardamom seeds; 3 cloves; and small cinnamon stick
1 bottle of Burgundy wine
Half a bottle of gin
40g seedless raisins
50g sugar

GLASS

Punch glass or tumbler

STEPS

1 - Pour the burgundy and half the gin into a saucepan and add the raisins and sugar.

2 - Add the bag of spices and cover before slowly bringing to the boil and then allowing to simmer for 30 minutes.

3 - Add the rest of the gin and remove from the heat.

4 - Remove the bag of spices and immediately ignite and serve.

Martini
and
Brandy

Apple Martini

This delicious cocktail is perfect to just sit down with and sip on a warm summer evening. It is light, refreshing and fruity. It is great to serve at a relaxed barbecue but is also stylish enough for a more formal occasion. There has been a real growth in popularity in recent years for fruit flavoured martinis as an alternative to the classic martini recipe. And while many tasty fruit variations exist, the apple martini is certainly my firm favourite.

INGREDIENTS
50 ml vodka
25 ml apple schnapps
25 ml apple juice

GLASS
Martini glass

GARNISH
Apple slice, cut thinly

STEPS
1 - Put a few ice cubes in the cocktail shaker.

2 - Add all of your ingredients.

3 - Put the lid on and shake well for roughly 20 seconds or so.

4 - Strain into the martini glass.

5 - Garnish with the apple slice.

TIP FROM THE BAR
For a more concentrated and sharp taste, you can leave out the apple juice and add a good splash of lemon or lime juice

Espresso Martini

A favourite drink of mine, this is great for starting an evening off with a kick. This creamy, velvety, almost dessert like cocktail is also a great alternative to the traditional after dinner coffee. The espresso martini has really taken off in the last few years, with many establishments coming up with their own twist on the original recipe. Variations, particularly those including chocolate are especially popular and will be detailed below.

INGREDIENTS
50 ml vodka
25 ml coffee liqueur
50 ml crème de cacao
50 ml espresso

GLASS
Martini glass

GARNISH
3 coffee beans

STEPS
1 - Put a few ice cubes in the cocktail shaker.

2 - Add all of your ingredients.

3 - Put the lid on and shake well for roughly 20 seconds or so.

4 - Strain into the martini glass.

5 - Garnish with the 3 coffee beans by placing them in the centre in an arrangement of a 3 petal flower.

TIP FROM THE BAR
For a more creamy and dessert like variation, instead of 50 ml of crème de cacao, use 50 ml of Bailey's Irish Cream.

Vesper Martini

The Vesper Martini was invented in Ian Fleming's *Casino Royale* by his fictional character, James Bond. He orders the following from the barman: 'Three measures of Gordon's, one of vodka, half a measure of Kina Lillet. Shake it very well until it's ice-cold, then add a large thin slice of lemon peel. Got it?' In the next chapter he names it after meeting Vesper Lynd. A fantastic take on a classic drink for those in a 007 mood.

INGREDIENTS
3 measures of gin
1 measure of vodka
Half measure of Kina Lillet

GLASS
Deep champagne goblet

GARNISH
Lemon peel

STEPS
1 - Take cocktail shaker and fill with ice.

2 - Add the gin, vodka and Kina Lillet.

3 - Shake vigorously for 5 seconds.

4 - Strain in to the glass.

5 - Add the lemon twist to the glass.

TIP FROM THE BAR
Although he does not specify the type of vodka, he does suggest to the barman after trying the drink that a 'vodka made with grain instead of potatoes' would be preferable.

Vodka Martini

A martini is one of the best known cocktails with unknown origins. A vodka martini is not a true martini according to purists - this has to made with gin. The vodka martini has also been known as a kangaroo and a vodkatini. Made famous by Ian Flemming's James Bond a vodka martini is simple to make and easy to enjoy!

INGREDIENTS
5 ml dry vermouth
3 measures vodka

GLASS
Deep champagne goblet

GARNISH
Green olive

STEPS
1 - Take a cocktail shaker and fill with ice.

2 - Take the glass and add the dry vermouth; swill for a few seconds.

3 - Add the vodka to the cocktail shaker and shake vigorously for 5 seconds.

4 - Strain the vodka in to the glass.

5 - Add a green olive and serve.

TIP FROM THE BAR
As with many martinis, the ratio of vodka to dry vermouth has varied hugely over the years. 1:1 ratios at the turn of the century have given way to 50:1 and 100:1.

Porn Star Marini

This international favourite is a vodka-based martini created in the 1990s by Douglas Ankra of LAB in London's Soho. It has a great mix of sweet and tart flavours and can be adapted for a variety of palates, both by the mixologist and the drinker. The shot of bubbly served on the side can be enjoyed before, during or after the cocktail to clear the palate, or mixed in if you prefer. One version I've enjoyed even had the fresh passion fruit served in it's own shot glass. It's great after work, before dinner or even with lighter desserts.

INGREDIENTS

35 ml vanilla vodka
15 ml passion fruit liqueur
25 ml passion fruit puree
15 ml vanilla syrup or 2 teaspoon vanilla sugar
50 ml bubbly (champagne, prosecco or similar) served separately
Half a fresh passion fruit

GLASS

Martini Glass plus a shot glass

GARNISH

½ fresh passion fruit floating on top

STEPS

1 - Add the first 4 ingredients into a cocktail shaker and top with ice.

2 - Shake vigorously.

3 - Pour through a cocktail strainer into a chilled martini glass.

4 - Cut a fresh passion fruit in half and gently float it on top.

5 - Pour the bubbly into a chilled shot glass and serve on the side.

TIPS FROM THE BAR

Variations can be made as follows:

Sprinkle vanilla sugar onto the cut passion fruit half and spoon it into a small shot glass. Add 10 ml lime juice to the cocktail shaker mix for a more tart flavour. A splash of pressed apple for a little more mellow flavour

Antonio's Martini

There is probably no drink with more variations than the martini. Vodka or gin, lemon or olive, apple or espresso – there is a flavour for everyone. Invented in America, the drink's popularity exploded when James Bond first appeared on our screens and ordered his "shaken not stirred".

We prefer a very simple version in our house, made with chilled vodka and a splash of vermouth. Winston Churchill was said to whisper the word 'vermouth' to a freshly poured glass of gin – we don't add much more than that!

It is an ideal drink to start the evening on, served with a light savoury snack such as cheese on toast, nuts, or olives. It's also a great way to finish an evening, all by itself.

INGREDIENTS
A bottle of chilled vodka, kept in the freezer
A splash of dry vermouth
Peel from a lemon

GLASS
Martini glass, chilled in the freezer for an hour prior to serving

STEPS
1 - Take one martini glass, chilled and slightly frosty for best results.

2 - Add a splash of vermouth.

3 - Fill the glass to the rim with ice cold vodka.

4 - Peel a slice of lemon peel.

5 - Gently run the lemon peel around the rim of the glass, then slide it into the glass.

Lychee Martini

This trendier variation of the martini cocktail has become a classic, as aperitif or just as a cocktail. It is loved for its freshness and exotic sweetness.

INGREDIENTS
100 ml lychee liqueur
600 ml vodka
300 ml gin
1 peeled lychee (fresh or canned)
Crushed ice

GLASS
A martini glass

STEPS
1 - Add the liquids together with crushed ice into a cocktail shaker.

2 - Shake.

3 - Pour into a Martini glass without the ice.

Port and Brandy

In cold weather, hot drinks aren't the only path to inner warmth. Someone once told me how they came to find this little gem of a drink when they went horse racing in the depth of winter to a small little meeting with their cousin who was a jockey at the time. He went off to the warmth of the weighing room and on tap mugs of tea saying, 'I will meet you here after the last race'.

Well, she was not sure where to go but soon found out there was not much option apart from the parade ring, betting and stands to watch the race and a very small bar with one large radiator, so that is the order of her route repeated four times. By the time she completed the first circuit and found the bar she was absolutely freezing and asked the barman what he had that could warm her up and he advised Port and Brandy, mixed together in the same glass and she found that this really did warm you from inside out. After 4 circuits, no food she forgot to meet her cousin and he had to come and find her!

It is amazing that since then she asked for this drink at pubs and restaurants and how many actually brought them out in separate glasses and when she asked for a bigger one and mixed them together got some funny looks.

Ingredients

30 ml brandy
30 ml tawny port
1 tablespoon lemon juice
1 teaspoon maraschino liqueur

GLASS

Brandy glass

GARNISH

Slice of orange

STEPS

1 - Add all the ingredients into a cocktail shaker.

2 - Add ice.

3 - Shake and then strain in a brandy glass with ice cubes.

4 - Stir well, garnish with a slice of orange and serve.

Queimada

Queimada is a punch made from Galician augardente (Orujo Galiego) – a spirit distilled from wine and flavoured with special herbs or coffee, plus sugar, lemon peel, coffee beans and cinnamon. Typically, while preparing the punch a spell or incantation is recited, so that special powers are conferred to the queimada and those drinking it.

INGREDIENTS
Orujo Gallego (a pomace brandy)
White sugar
Coffee beans
Lemon peel
Cinnamon

GLASS
A brandy glass

STEPS
1 - In a bowl of clay is poured the brandy and sugar in the proportion of 120 grams per litre of liquid, adding lemon peels and coffee beans to the mixture.

2 - The mixture needs to be stirred with a dipper in that you previously have placed some sugar with brandy and set alight. We approach the dipper to the container very slowly until the fire pass from one to another. Stir until the sugar is consumed.

3 - In the same dipper pour some sugar, this time dry, and placing it on the queimada moves it until it becomes syrup which is poured on the flames and stirring wait for the flames and stirring, wait for the flames to get a bluish colour.

4 - The shorter the burn, the stronger the queimada.

Pisco Sour

Pisco is a strong South American brandy, made from certain varieties of grapes which are fermented and distilled. It is said that Pisco came into being as a way of using up the grapes leftover from wine making after it was introduced to South America by the Spanish. Pisco is produced in Chile and Peru: both countries claiming to be the original producers. The first Pisco sour cocktail is said to have been invented by an American, Victor Morris, in the 1920s at the Morris Bar in Lima, Peru.

INGREDIENTS
90 ml Pisco (grape brandy)
30 ml simple (sugar) syrup
30 ml lime juice
1 egg white
Angostura bitters (2/3 dashes)
Ice cubes

GLASS
Any old-fashioned looking glass

STEPS
1 - Mix the Pisco, lime juice, syrup and egg white in a cocktail shaker.

2 - Add the ice to fill the cocktail shaker and shake well for about 30 seconds.

3 - Serve strained into an old-fashioned glass and sprinkle the Angostura bitters on top of the foam.

TIP FROM THE BAR
When the Pisco sour is poured into a glass, there should be at least half an inch of foam on the top of the glass. The bitters are sprinkled onto them.

Incredible Hulk

This cocktail is named after the comic book superhero and can describe any alcoholic drink which is bright green in colour. The version described below became popular just after the millennium and uses Hpnotiq as its base liqueur. Hpnotiq is made from fruit juices, vodka and a cognac but it is bright blue rather than green. Unfortunately, its colour made it unpopular with male drinkers but once combined with Hennessy it turns bright green. The resultant powerful green cocktail gained universal appeal among drinkers.

INGREDIENTS
20 ml Hennessy cognac
20 ml Hpnotiq liqueur

GLASS
Any small glass

STEPS
1 - Chill both the beverages before use.

2 - In a cocktail shaker with ice, combine the Hennessy cognac and the Hpnotiq until it turns bright green in colour.

3 - Shake and strain into a small rocks glass with ice.

4 - Serve.

Brandy Alexander

After a good dinner, you may not want a dessert but a sweet drink with a difference is a fine way to finish an evening.

INGREDIENTS

2 parts brandy
1 part crème de cacao
2 parts double cream
A pinch of grated nutmeg

GLASS

A wide champagne glass

GARNISH

Nutmeg

STEPS

1 - Pour the brandy, crème de cacao and double cream into a cocktail shaker.

2 - Top up with crushed ice and shake well.

3 - Pour into champagne glass.

4 - Sprinkle with a little nutmeg and serve.

Gin

Gin and Tonic - Three Versions with a Twist

G&T. I love those two letters. My favourite drink. G&T. Gin and tonic. Refreshingly nice and distinctive, versatile in its sweet and sourness. No other drink can compete against its subtle or strong bitterness, depending on how you refine the gin and tonic ratio.

Having a gin and tonic in my hand makes me feel like me. In the late evening it makes me reflect on the day and helps me clear my mind. Running out of the ingredients gets me running to the shops quicker than running out of almost anything else.

On a recent birthday, my wife surprised me with delicious versions of G&T which I had never tried before. She chose them to accompany the birthday dinner and hired a bartender to mix them for our guests and us.

I would like to introduce you to three versions. My wife named them: Mr Green; Mr Purple; and Mr Tea. The 'Mister' comes from her thought of G&Ts as a very manly drink.

They are a party hit, as people usually know a G&T but are not familiar adding additional flavours to it. A little more preparation is required than for a classic G&T but they are certainly not difficult to make.

Gin and Tonic: Mr Green:

This version is perfect for any starters, for seafood or on its own as a refreshing drink in high summer.

INGREDIENTS:

50 ml gin
100 ml tonic water
4 cucumber slices
1 sprig of rosemary
Juice of a couple of lime wedges
20 ml sparkling water
Ice cubes

GLASS

Highball tumbler

GARNISH

Rosemary and Lime wedge

STEPS

1 - Cut the cucumber slices in quarters and place at the bottom of the glass.

2 - Cover with freshly squeezed lime juice.

3 - Add a small piece of the Rosemary sprig and slightly muddle the cucumber, while carefully allowing the Rosemary to let off some flavour.

4 - Add the remaining sprig of Rosemary and fill the glass with ice cubes.

5 - Add the Gin, tonic and finish off with sparkling water.

Gin and Tonic: Mr Purple

This version has a jammy, berry flavour and combines well with a hearty main course like any dark red meat. On its own it works well as a winter drink.

INGREDIENTS:

50 ml gin
120 ml tonic water
Splash cassis
Ice cubes

GLASS

Highball tumbler

GARNISH

Lime wedge

STEPS

1 - Fill the glass with Ice cubes.

2 - Add a splash of cassis. Be careful not to use too much as cassis has quite a pronounced presence.

3 - Now add the gin, give it one stir.

4 - Fill the glass up with tonic water.

Gin and Tonic: Mr Tea

This version is excellent with any kind of dessert! No need to have a dessert with it, though, you can also finish off your meal with this drink on its own!

INGREDIENTS:
50 ml gin
30 ml cold English breakfast tea or earl grey
Splash elderflower cordial or 10 ml elderflower Liqueur
75 ml tonic water
Splash freshly squeezed lemon
Ice cubes

GLASS
Highball tumbler

GARNISH
Slice of lemon

STEPS
1 - Pour the gin, tea and elderflower cordial (or liqueur) into a cocktail shaker, squeeze in a bit of fresh lemon, add a few ice cubes and shake well.

2 - Fill the tumbler with ice cubes and add the mixture from the cocktail shaker.

3 - Fill up with tonic water.

4 - Garnish with slice of lemon.

Hanky Panky

Celebrating our silver wedding anniversary last year with a weekend in London, my wife and I treated ourselves with afternoon tea at the Savoy Hotel before we went to the theatre. We enjoyed this immensely and in our opinion it was much superior than the afternoon tea served at the Ritz.

After this we had a bit of time to kill so we decided to visit the American Bar, the famous cocktail bar in the Savoy. I always have a dilemma when choosing what to order so I asked the bartender's recommendation and he suggested a Hanky Panky. The name would normally have put me off the drink as I would feel awkward asking for one with lurid connotations.

The bartender explained that the drink was first made in the American Bar by the then head bartender Ada Coleman for the actor Charles Hawtrey in the 1920s. When he first tasted it he exclaimed 'By jove! That is the real hanky panky!' It has been known as hanky panky ever since and it certainly hits the spot!

INGREDIENTS
1 measure gin
1 measure sweet vermouth
2 dashes Fernet Branca
Ice cubes

GLASS
Cocktail glass

GARNISH
An orange twist

STEPS

1 - Stir ingredients well in a mixing glass.

2 - Strain into a chilled glass.

3 - Twist a small slice of orange peel over the surface of the drink.

4 - Serve and enjoy.

Tom Collins

A long summer drink, ideal for sipping in the sunshine. Theories as to the origin of the name are many but it seems unlikely that there ever was an eponymous Tom Collins. However, this classic has been known since at least 1876 when it was mentioned in Jerry Thomas' *Bartender's Guide*. Below is the recipe for the original sour drink, with the option of adding extra sugar to taste

INGREDIENTS

12 ice cubes
60 ml gin
20 ml freshly squeezed lemon juice
1 to 4 teaspoons of brown sugar
Soda water

GLASS

A chilled Collins glass

GARNISH

2 slices of lemon

STEPS

1 - Place 3 or 4 ice cubes in a chilled glass, followed by the lemon slices and 3 or 4 more cubes of ice.

2 - Add the gin, lemon juice, sugar and 4 or 5 ice cubes to a cocktail shaker.

3 - Shake until cold.

4 - Strain into the glass.

5 - Top up with soda water and stir.

TIPS FROM THE BAR

Try replacing the gin with rum, tequila, vodka or whisky.

Singapore Sling

This refreshing long cocktail was devised by a bartender working in the iconic Raffles Hotel in Singapore at the start of the 20th Century. There is much dispute over the authenticity of different recipes but I find this one to be a very pleasing replica of one I was lucky enough to sample on my honeymoon there in 2004.

INGREDIENTS

Juice of half a lemon
80 ml pineapple juice
30 ml gin
15 ml cherry brandy
7 ml triple sec (or Cointreau would do)
Dash angostura bitters
Soda water to taste

GLASS

Tall tumbler

GARNISH

Cocktail cherry
Slice of lemon

STEPS

1 - Half fill a cocktail shaker with ice.

2 - Add all the ingredients except the soda and shake.

3 - Strain into a tall glass.

4 - Add a few ice cubes and top up with soda water.

5 - Decorate with a cocktail cherry and slice of lemon if required.

Gin Fizz

Fizzes originated in America early in the 20th Century, particularly in the Deep South where they proved very popular. The gin fizz is the best known of this style of drink, and is said to be particularly good drunk in the morning, although I would only recommend this if you have a clear afternoon!

INGREDIENTS

15 ml sugar syrup
Juice of 1 lemon
50 ml gin
Soda water

GLASS

Tall glass

STEPS

1 - Half fill a cocktail shaker with ice.

2 - Add all the ingredients except the soda and shake well.

3 - Strain into a tall glass and top up with soda water.

4 - Serve and enjoy.

TIPS FROM THE BAR

This should be drunk as soon as prepared in order to retain the flavour. Although not authentic, lime juice makes a tasty alternative to the lemon.

Paradise

A classic aperitif best taken before dinner. This cocktail owes its origins to Harry Craddock, an American barman working at the Savoy Hotel in London between the wars.

INGREDIENTS

40 ml gin
20 ml apricot brandy
30 ml freshly squeezed orange juice

GLASS

A chilled cocktail glass

GARNISH

A cherry

STEPS

1 - Add the liquid ingredients and 4-5 ice cubes to a cocktail shaker.

2 - Shake until cold.

3 - Strain into a chilled glass.

4 - Add a cherry as garnish.

TIPS FROM THE BAR

The amount of orange juice can be increased from the standard recipe if more sweetness is required.

Alexander

It is likely that this gin-based cocktail was invented in prohibition era New York, as a refreshing white cocktail. Since that time it has been adapted using other spirits as a base, but this remains an elegant short drink which benefits greatly from vigorous shaking, entrapping air and giving a light feel on the tongue.

INGREDIENTS

30 ml gin
30 ml crème de cacao liqueur
30 ml single cream

GLASS

Sour glass

GARNISH

A pinch of ground nutmeg

STEPS

1 - Add all the ingredients and 4 to 5 ice cubes to a cocktail shaker.

2 - Shake vigorously.

3 - Pour into chilled glass.

4 - Add a sprinkle of nutmeg for decoration.

The Pinky

This simple, thrills free, gin-based drink finds itself a favourite amongst the sporting members of Oxford University. It is a refreshing drink that is easy to make and even easier to drink, making it the ideal choice for escalating proceedings on a night out with friends. Not to be taken lightly.

INGREDIENTS

100 ml gin
Half a lemon
Orange juice
Monin grenadine mixer

GLASS

Pint glass

STEPS

1 - Take one pint glass and add a few ice cubes.

2 - Add 50 ml of gin, and squeeze the juice of half a lemon into the glass.

3 - Add 175 ml of orange juice and gently stir.

4 - Add a further 50 ml of gin and another 175 ml of orange juice.

5 - Again, gently stir.

6 - Fill to the top with grenadine and enjoy.

Negroni

This is a European classic originated from northern Italy. This cocktail is easy to prepare and can be served as an aperitif.

INGREDIENTS

300 ml gin
300 ml vermouth rosso
300 ml Campari
Ice cubes

GLASS

Tumbler

GARNISH

Orange peel

STEPS

1- Add all ingredients into a tumbler and stir.

2 - Add the orange peel for decoration.

3 - Serve and enjoy.

Colony

A legendary 1920s cocktail that has survived the test of time and hits the spot just as well today as it did during the days of Prohibition.

INGREDIENTS

40 ml gin
20 ml grapefruit juice
6 ml maraschino liqueur

GLASS

Large highball glass

GARNISH

Grapefruit slices
Mint leaves

STEPS

1- Pour the gin, grapefruit juice and Maraschino liqueur into a pint glass.

2 - Shake well.

3 - Pour the drink into a glass filled with ice.

4 - Garnish with a couple of grapefruit slices and mint leaves.

Rum
and
Bacardi

Piña Colada

The piña Ccolada was invented in August 1954 at the Caribe Hilton's Beachcomber Bar in San Juan, Puerto Rico by its alleged creator, Ramon 'Monchito' Marrero. The hotel wanted Monchito to mix a new signature drink. Monchito accepted the challenge, and after three intense months of blending, shaking and experimenting, the first piña colada was born.

INGREDIENTS

330 ml rum
1 tablespoon coconut rum
40 ml coconut cream
40 ml pineapple juice
3 pineapple chunks

GLASS

Cocktail glass

GARNISH

Cherry

STEPS

1 - Put all ingredients into a blender and blend until smooth.

2 - Pour into a cocktail glass.

3 - Garnish with a cherry.

Flaming Dr Pepper

This mix is supposed to taste like Dr Pepper and can be made a couple of different ways. It's common that the shot of liqueur is lit aflame then dropped into a half glass of lager, but some will also make it by placing the shot glass filled with liquor into the larger glass, after which the beer is poured around the edges, just to the rim and the liquor is lit. Whichever way you choose to pour your Flaming Dr Pepper, remember to blow out the flame prior to consumption and, as with any flaming drink, be careful.

INGREDIENTS

25 ml amaretto liqueur
7 ml strong rum
560 ml lager

GLASS

Shot glass
Pint glass

STEPS

1 - Fill a shot glass three-quarters full with amaretto.

2 - Slowly float the strong rum to fill the glass.

3 - Fill a pint glass with lager.

4 - Ignite the contents of the shot glass.

5 - Blow out the flame, drop the shot glass into the lager.

Bacardi

This simple but delicious cocktail is a personal favourite of mine. Easy to prepare, and very easy to drink! But beware; a law was passed in America back in the 1930s – only authentic Bacardi white rum should be used to make them.

INGREDIENTS

20 ml lime juice
50 ml Bacardi
7 to 10 ml grenadine (depending on personal preference)

GLASS

Rum glass

STEPS

1 - Half fill a cocktail shaker with ice.

2 - Add all the ingredients.

3 - Shake well, and strain into a cocktail glass.

Prohibition

Pink and fruity, the perfect drink for those with a sweet tooth. A great drink for a hot summer's day.

INGREDIENTS

50 ml Bacardi
30 ml pineapple juice
10 ml grenadine
20 ml maraschino liqueur

GLASS

Cocktail glass

STEPS

1 - Pour the pineapple juice, grenadine, Maraschino liqueur and Bacardi into a pint glass.

2 - Fill a shaker with ice cubes and add the cocktail – shake well.

3 - Strain the cocktail into a glass and serve.

Mojito

The mojito cocktail traditionally originates from Cuba. The first version of the drink was actually meant as remedy to fight off tropical illnesses obviously it was not called a mojito at this time but soon became popular as the mint, lime and sugar hid the strong taste of rum. The mojito which now comes in many different versions and flavours, yet the classic mojito is the most refreshing of drinks especially on a warm summers night.

INGREDIENTS

70 ml light white rum
One and a half limes sliced into wedges
2-3 spoons granulated white sugar
2 dozen fresh mint leaves
Handful of ice
Soda water to taste

GLASS

Tumbler

GARNISH

Fresh mint leaves

STEPS

1 - Use a strong tall glass to bruise the limes, mint and sugar to release the flavours. You can use the end of wide rolling pin to do this.

2 - Add a handful of ice followed by the rum.

3 - Add soda water to taste.

4 - Garnish with the fresh mint leaves.

Daiquiri

Daiquiri is a small town in Cuba, where this drink is said to have originated from. It is refreshing, light and perfect for summer.

INGREDIENTS
60 ml Koko Kanu (coconut rum)
30 ml fresh lime juice
1 teaspoon sugar syrup

GLASS
1 chilled cocktail glass

GARNISH
1 lime slice

STEPS
1 - Place the rum, lime juice and sugar syrup into a cocktail shaker.

2 - Shake well for 20 seconds.

3 - Pour into a chilled cocktail glass.

4 - Garnish with a slice of lime.

TIP FROM THE BAR
To make sugar syrup, mix 30 ml cold water and 1.5 tablespoons of sugar, place in a bottle and shake until the sugar has completely dissolved. Why not try a frozen fruit daiquiri? Simply add crushed ice and a handful of fresh strawberries at stage one and blend all of the ingredients until slushy, garnish with a strawberry and enjoy. I also recommend passion fruit and mango.

Vodka
and
Tequila

Vodka Sundowner

Traditionally served at sunset to signify the end of the working day, the sundowner is the perfect accompaniment to end a hot summers day with friends. Though originally introduced by the British, these vodka based cocktails have become an African tradition, originally being served to hunters in the 1920s. They now however are a welcome 'end of the day' beverage to relax tourists and dwellers alike globally after a busy day.

The sundowner is the perfect cocktail to have fun with friends on summers days, sampling each other's unique flavours and smiling together as the sun goes down. Think fine dining on roof terraces, late afternoon BBQs with friends, beach front villas watching the sunset to name just a few. The Sundowner is a sublime way to conclude the day just spent.

INGREDIENTS

50 ml of vodka
1 dash of raspberry syrup
1 small bottle (160 ml) of fresh orange juice
Ice cubes
Long spoon

GLASS

Highball glass

GARNISH

Orange twist on glass

STEPS

1- Place ice cubes in the highball glass.

2 - Measure two shots of vodka and pour over the ice cubes.

3 - Open the orange juice and pour juice over the ice cubes.

4 - Place the long spoon into the glass.

5 - Pour a dash of raspberry syrup over the back of the spoon.

6 - Add an orange twist to the glass, relax and enjoy!

TIP FROM THE BAR

Why not try experimenting with different flavours of syrups, exchanging vodka for rum, adding lemon juice or perhaps sampling grenadine for a different sundowner twist?

Vodka Sunrise

The stresses of a family Christmas morning disappeared completely as we tried this cocktail as part of our breakfast. Whilst it is tempting, it is not recommended for the cook to have too many! It is just as memorable sitting outside on those warm summer evenings with either good company or a good book.

INGREDIENTS

5 ml grenadine
1 part vodka
2 parts fresh orange juice

GLASS

Tall tumbler

GARNISH

Slices of lemon and/or orange

STEPS

1 - Slowly pour the grenadine into a chilled glass avoiding the sides.

2 - In a separate glass, stir the vodka and orange juice with crushed ice.

3 - Strain vodka mix into the grenadine glass so it splashes on to the grenadine.

4 - Garnish with lemon and/or orange.

Moscow Mule

The Moscow mule was originally conceived in the United States rather than Russia as its name suggests. It was the brainchild of John G. Martin, who, in 1946, was responsible for Smirnoff in the US. During a visit to Hollywood's Cock 'n' Bull pub, John spoke with its owner Jack Morgan about his desire to increase Smirnoff's popularity. Jack was keen to promote his Cock 'n' Bull ginger beer and so the vodka and ginger beer combination was created. The cocktail was named after the capital of vodka's homeland, Moscow, and an antiquated term for ginger beer, mule. With its catchy name, and ease to make, it's no wonder that this refreshing cocktail came to popularise vodka in the US.

INGREDIENTS

50 ml vodka
200 ml ginger beer
The juice of one lime

GLASS

Highball glass

GARNISH

Fresh mint

STEPS

1 - Squeeze the lime juice into a highball glass and add ice.

2 - Pour over the vodka and finally the ginger beer.

3 - Stir the ingredients and garnish with a sprig of fresh mint to serve.

TIP FROM THE BAR

Ginger ale could be used as an alternative to ginger beer.

Stinger

This is an old recipe I learned from my Swedish friends. It is basically a grown up shot – the perfect antidote to the sweet and nasty shots that have become *de rigeur* for today's adolescents. In typical Swedish style, the ingredients and manufacture are simple, but need to be planned. Perfect out of the fridge, sip it slowly, either after dinner or at the end of an evening.

INGREDIENTS

1 bottle vodka
1 bag salt liquorice (available from specialist outlets)

GLASS

Shot glass

STEPS

1 - Add the salt liquorice to the vodka.

2 - Leave for 4 to 7 days to dissolve and infuse.

3 - Pour and enjoy.

TIP FROM THE BAR

You may need to do some trial and error to get the intensity to your particular taste. The more liquorice and the longer you leave it, the stronger the taste.

Cosmopolitan

The cosmopolitan still enjoys international favour after reaching its celebrity peak in the 1990s, thanks to Madonna and the girls in television's *Sex and the City*. The origins of the modern 'cosmo' are disputed, most hotly by bartenders in Miami and Minneapolis; but its origin may date back to the early 1900s when gin was used instead of vodka. Served up in a martini glass, it has succeeded by appealing to the both eyes and the taste buds of the patrons of after-work bars and nightclubs.

INGREDIENTS
40 ml vodka (citrus vodka is a common choice)
15 ml Cointreau or triple sec liqueur
15 ml fresh lime juice
30 ml cranberry juice

GLASS
Martini glass

GARNISH
Slice of lime or a flamed orange twist

STEPS
1 - Add all 4 ingredients into a cocktail shaker and top with ice.

2 - Shake vigorously.

3 - Pour through a cocktail strainer into a chilled martini glass.

4 - Garnish (take care if flaming your orange twist).

5 - Serve immediately for the desired pink frothy appearance.

TIP FROM THE BAR
Different flavoured vodkas can be used for subtle changes whilst many larger variations have been made by substituting the liqueur and/or the cranberry with different flavours.

Woo Woo

The origins of this cocktail and its name is the stuff of legend. Some say it originated in 1950s New York, others say its origin coincided with the world series of baseball in the 1980s. Every time the NY Mets hit a home run, the people in the bar shouted 'Woo Woo!' Whatever its beginnings, this cocktail is a sweet reminder of the versatility of vodka. It is best shared with friends at a sporting event.

INGREDIENTS

25 ml vodka
25 ml peach schnapps
75 ml cranberry juice

GLASS

Highball glass

GARNISH

Slice of lime

STEPS

1 - Take a cocktail shaker and add 25 ml of vodka.

2 - Add 25 ml of peach schnapps followed by 75 ml of cranberry juice.

3 - Shake well for 5 to 10 seconds.

4 - Pour into highball glass filled with ice.

5 - Garnish with a slice of lime on side of glass.

Bay Breeze

The bay breeze is a derivative of the sea breeze, which as a cocktail was born near the end of the Prohibition era. The sea breeze has undergone several evolutions, finally settling in its current form in the 1960s. The bay breeze substitutes pineapple juice for grapefruit. It is a refreshing cocktail, ideally suited to winding down after a summer's walk along the beach.

INGREDIENTS

25 ml vodka
25 ml cranberry juice
75 ml pineapple juice

GLASS

Highball glass

GARNISH

Slice of lime or pineapple wedge

STEPS

1 - Take a highball glass and fill with ice.

2 - Pour in the pineapple juice, followed by the cranberry juice.

3 - Add the vodka.

4 - Stir well for 5 to 10 seconds.

5 - Garnish with a slice of lime or pineapple wedge on side of glass.

Chi Chi

Hawaii claims this variation of Puerto Rica's piña colada, substituting vodka as the base instead of rum. This is a sweet and refreshing long drink ideal for sipping outside on a hot summer's evening.

INGREDIENTS
60 ml vodka
30 ml coconut cream
120 ml pineapple juice
2 scoops of crushed ice (or ice cream)

GLASS
A highball glass

GARNISH
A slice of pineapple and a maraschino cherry

STEPS
1 - Add the ingredients into a blender.

2 - Blend until smooth.

3 - Decant into a cooled glass.

4 - Add pineapple slice and cherry as garnish.

TIP FROM THE BAR
A scoop of vanilla ice cream can be added for a sweeter (and more calorific) finish.

Screwdriver

A screwdriver makes a great summer fruit juice cocktail with an added punch of vodka.

INGREDIENTS

50 ml vodka
50 ml orange juice (or to fill)
Ice

GLASS

Tumbler glass

GARNISH

Orange slices

STEPS

1 - Add ice to a tumbler.

2 - Pour two parts vodka to two parts orange juice over ice.

3 - Stir well.

4 - Garnish with an orange wedge.

The Big Apple

Much like the city it is named after, this drink has everything you need to get the party going.

INGREDIENTS
40 ml apple vodka
Lemonade
A fresh lime

GLASS
Collins glass

GARNISH
A slice of apple

STEPS
1 - Fill the glass with ice cubes.

2 - Pour in the green apple vodka.

3 - Fill to the top with lemonade.

4 - Squeeze in fresh lime and drop into drink.

5 - Serve with a slice of apple as a garnish.

Long Island Ice Tea

This long drink is internationally recognized and famed for its potency. Competing claims for creating this drink date from Long Island, Tennessee in Prohibition era 1920s and Long Island, New York in the 1970s Disco era. With the benign appearance of black tea, a gently refreshing taste and an alcohol content typically 22% abv, it is easy to see why this drink could be popular in these times and remains so now. It is best enjoyed in the evening and in a limited number.

INGREDIENTS

15 ml vodka
15 ml gin
15 ml tequila
15 ml white rum
15 ml triple sec (or Cointreau)
25 ml fresh lemon juice
30 ml sugar syrup
1 dash of cola

GLASS

Highball/Collins Glass

GARNISH

Lemon slice or wedge

STEPS

1 - Half fill a highball glass with ice.

2 - Add all ingredients and stir gently.

3 - Garnish and serve.

TIPS FROM THE BAR

Half the fresh lemon juice can be substituted with fresh lime juice.

Beach Blast

A fine drink for a beautifully sunny evening when you want to loosen up and let off some steam. Guaranteed to help barbecues go with a swing!

INGREDIENTS

50 ml tequila
125 ml orange juice
25 ml Galliano

GLASS

Highball glass

STEPS

1 - Fill the highball glass with ice cubes.

2 - Add 50 ml of tequila to the glass, pouring over the ice.

3 - Pour in the orange Juice until the glass is three-quarters full.

4 - Pour in slowly and carefully over a teaspoon 25 ml of Galliano on top of the drink.

6 - Garnish with a lemon wedge on the side of the glass.

The Stamfordian

A supremely refreshing gentleman's drink for the modern man. Satisfying when enjoyed in a bar, even more satisfying enjoyed back at hers.

INGREDIENTS

25 ml tequila
10 ml Mandarine Napoleon (orange liqueur)
20 ml fresh lime juice
One scoop of honeybutter
One scoop of lemon sorbet

GLASS

Martini glass

STEPS

1 - Take one pint glass and add a small scoop of honeybutter (prepared by blending together honey with some creamy butter).

2 - Dilute with a shot of tequila and stir.

3 - Add a bar spoon of lemon sorbet and give a nice stir to break it all down and let it all melt so that it looks nice and creamy.

4 - Add a taste (about 10 ml) of Mandarine Napoleon (orange liqueur).

5 - Add around 15 to 20 ml of freshly squeezed lime.

6 - Finally, add some cubed ice and shake well, before serving in a chilled, stemmed martini glass.

Mexican Summer

The taste of a Mexican summer in a glass.

INGREDIENTS
25 ml tequila
12 ml Grand Mariner
12 ml sugar syrup
12 ml pure orange juice
50 ml cranberry juice
Squeeze of fresh lime

GLASS
Highball glass

GARNISH
Lime wedge

STEPS
1 - Pour all ingredients into a cocktail shaker and add ice.

2 - Shake well.

3 - Strain into a chilled highball glass and garnish with a lime wedge.

Whisky

Whisky Sour

The whisky sour has been around for over a hundred years, and traditionally includes some combination of whisky, lemon juice and sugar, served either straight or over ice. My family is from Vermont, and decided to give this classic a little makeover, replacing the sugar with a Vermont staple – maple syrup.

INGREDIENTS

60 ml whisky
50 ml maple syrup
1 lemon (juice only)

GLASS

Best served in a crystal tumbler

STEPS

1 - Take one tumbler and add a handful of ice cubes.
2 - Add 60 ml of whisky.
3 - Add 50 ml of maple syrup.
4 - Squeeze juice of 1 lemon over the drink.
5 - Stir well to combine.

The Boilermaker

The boilermaker has the ability to get you drunk very quick, making it a popular party drink. When drinking dropped shots one needs to take care not to get too wild (although that's a rarity in this case). Shot glasses floating freely inside the bigger glass have been known to chip many teeth, so consider yourself warned. That hazard and the intoxicating effect of downing lager and whisky so quickly deems the boilermaker worthy of only the bravest (or craziest) of drinkers. It is deceptively alcoholic so please imbibe with caution.

INGREDIENTS
450 ml draft lager (lighter is best)
60 ml blended whisky

GLASS
Shot glass
Pint glass

STEPS
1 - Pour a shot of whisky in a shot glass.

2 - Fill a pint glass with lager.

3 - Drop the shot glass into the lager and down everything in one drink.

Four Horsemen

The Four Horsemen is a cocktail containing four hard liquors and named after the Four Horsemen of the Apocalypse. The name of the drink is derived from the fact that the most common brand names of each ingredient are also male given names and the drinks have a high alcohol content (and therefore tend to have a very strong effect on human physiology). Additionally, the four brand names usually all begin with the letter J giving further unity to the concept of the four horsemen.

INGREDIENTS
1 part bourbon whisky (e.g. Jim Beam)
1 part Tennessee whisky (e.g. Jack Daniels)
1 part Scotch whisky (e.g. Johnnie Walker Black)
1 part Irish whisky (e.g. Jameson)

GLASS
Shot glass

STEPS
1 - Pour a shot of each whisky into a shot glass.

2 - Best consumed in one gulp but if having more than one of these then beware of the high alcohol content.

Godfather

Sweet and warming. Contrary to popular belief this cocktail has no connection to the American crime film of the same name. The origin of this drink remains unknown.

INGREDIENTS
60 ml Scotch Whisky
60 ml Amaretto
5 ml orange juice (freshly squeezed)

GLASS
Tumbler

GARNISH
1 slice of orange

STEPS
1 - Fill the tumbler three-quarters full of ice.

2 - Add the whisky, Amaretto and orange juice and gently stir for 20 seconds until all of the alcohol has mixed.

3 - Garnish with a cold slice of orange and enjoy.

TIP FROM THE BAR
Rim the glass with sugar or salt to add an ascetically pleasing edge to your cocktail. Take a wedge of lemon, lime or orange (use which ever compliments your drink) and run it around the edge of your glass 3-4 times, tip the glass and dip it into either salt or sugar, easy!

Havana Cooler

During a long walk in Cuba, we came across a man selling machete peeled and sliced pineapple from his thatched shed - he recommended we get a Havana cooler in the first bar we came across in the next town. It is a drink for those lazy sunny Sunday afternoons.

INGREDIENTS
50 ml Havana Club (rum)
Ginger ale
2 ice cubes

GLASS
Tall tumbler

GARNISH
Pineapple and/or lemon and of course a sprig of mint

STEPS
1 - Mix rum and ice cubes in the glass.

2 - Top up with ginger ale and garnish.

3 - Stir and serve.

Rob Roy

The Rob Roy cocktail was invented in the Waldorf Astoria hotel in New York. It is named after legendary Scottish outlaw Rob Roy MacGregor. It is very similar to a Manhattan cocktail, but made with scotch whisky, not bourbon. My uncle was a hotelier in Scotland and although he himself was a teetotaller, he enjoyed making this cocktail for his visitors embellished of course with tales of the man himself.

INGREDIENTS
45 ml Scotch whisky
15 ml martini rosso
Dash angostura bitters

GLASS
Large glass

GARNISH
Maraschino cherry

STEPS
1 - Half fill glass with ice.

2 - Add the ingredients and stir well.

3 - Strain into a cocktail glass.

4 - Garnish with the cherry.

Churchill

Sir Winston Churchill allegedly created this cocktail on one of his many visits to the famous Savoy hotel. Bitter or sweet? You decide.

INGREDIENTS

50 ml Scotch whisky
10 ml vermouth (sweet)
10 ml triple sec
10 ml Cointreau
10 ml lime juice

GLASS

Chilled cocktail glass

GARNISH

1 slice of lime

STEPS

1 - Fill a cocktail shaker with ice cubes.

2 - Add all of the ingredients and stir gently for 30 to 40 seconds with a small spoon.

3 - Strain into a chilled cocktail glass.

4 - Garnish with a slice of lime.

TIP FROM THE BAR

Take a vegetable peeler and peel fruit rind to use as a garnish either in or on the glass. This is a simple but effective way to add an imaginative twist to any drink.

Old Fashioned

This is a classic cocktail to unwind with after a long day. Some would say that it is in fact *the* original cocktail. Dating back to the 1800s, this drink has a strong following. The recipe provided here is close to what is considered to be the original, although many variations, to the exasperation of the purists! It is a delicious and relaxing cocktail to enjoy as a nightcap or on a cold winter evening.

INGREDIENTS
50 ml bourbon or rye whisky
2 dashes of Angostura bitters
1 teaspoon of sugar syrup or 1 sugar cube

GLASS
Traditional tumbler, known as an old Fashioned glass

GARNISH
Orange or lemon peel

STEPS
1 - Pour the sugar syrup into your glass. If you are using the sugar cube instead of the syrup, put it in the glass and wet it with a few drops of water and press it with the mixer until it becomes a syrup.

2 - Pour the 2 dashes of the Angostura bitters in.

3 - Add your bourbon or rye whisky.

4 - Add ice according to taste. I prefer it with quite a bit of ice but there are those who prefer it with little or none at all.

5 - Stir lightly.

6 - Cut or peel a thin but long piece of orange or lemon peel, depending on which fruit you prefer. Place this in the glass.

Manhattan

This is a classic strong aperitif cocktail. It was created in a club in New York, which is where the name originates from.

INGREDIENTS
2 dash Angostura bitters
200 ml vermouth rosso
400 ml bourbon whisky
Ice cubes

GLASS
Martini glass

STEPS
1 - Add all the ingredients into a Martini glass.

2 - Stir and serve.

Jack and Coke

Also known as a JD and Coke, this drink is a cocktail made from Jack Daniels bourbon whisky and Coca Cola. The term Jack and Coke was an advertising slogan used when both products were marketed together for the first time.

INGREDIENTS
1 part Jack Daniels Tennessee whisky
3 parts Coca Cola
Ice cubes

GLASS
Collins glass

GARNISH
Lime or lemon wedge

STEPS
1 - Part fill a Collins glass with ice cubes.

2 - Add 1 part Jack Daniels Whisky.

3 - Add 3 parts Coca Cola.

4 - Stir and top up ice if necessary.

5 - Garnish with a lime or lemon wedge.

Coffees
and
Cream Liqueurs

Irish Coffee

It is hard to beat Irish Coffee which was invented and named by Joe Sheridan who worked at Foynes airport (the precursor to Shannon International) in the west of Ireland. Sheridan allegedly added whisky to coffee to warm waiting passengers. Sheridan named it Irish coffee.

INGREDIENTS

60 ml Irish whisky
1 or 2 teaspoons brown sugar
180 ml freshly-brewed strong black coffee
2 teaspoons heavy cream

GLASS

Stemmed whisky glass

STEPS

1 - Warm a teaspoon in a cup of hot water and leave it there until needed.

2 - Preheat a stemmed whisky glass or coffee cup with hot water, once warm discard the water.

3 - Add brown sugar to the glass or cup.

4 - Fill it with strong black coffee leaving 2 centimetres at the top.

5 - Stir gently until the sugar is completely dissolved (the sugar will ensure that the cream will float).

6 - Add the Irish Whisky and stir again.

7 - Let it sit until the mixture is perfectly still.

8 - Using the hot teaspoon, back side up and held close to the surface, gently pour the prepared cream over the back of the teaspoon and rest on top of the coffee layer.

9 - Gradually raise the spoon as you slowly pour in the cream. This will result in a layer of cream that floats on top of the coffee. What you should be left with is a glass of black coffee (not cloudy and with no trace of cream) with a white collar.

10 - Served on a side plate with no spoon.

TIPS FROM THE BAR

Do not stir it once made. Sipping the coffee through the cream will result in the best Irish coffee drinking experience.

Jamaican Coffee

A Jamaican Coffee is a coffee drink with a shot of Jamaican Rum and Tia Maria or Kahlua. It is a liquor coffee and is also known as a calypso coffee or Spanish coffee. It is served in a liquor coffee glass and topped up with fresh cream which floats on the top. It is usually served as an after dinner drink and is a Caribbean equivalent of the world famous Irish coffee. This would be a great drink to serve on a cold and chilly evening.

INGREDIENTS
1 glass of brewed black coffee
1 measure dark rum
1 measure Tia Maria or Kahlua liquor
Double or whipped cream

GLASS
Liquor coffee glass

GARNISH
1 coffee bean or ground allspice

STEPS
1 - Pour rum and liquor into a tall coffee glass.

2 - Fill to four fifths of the glass height with hot black coffee.

3 - Fill to the top with the cream.

4 - Garnish with the coffee bean or ground allspice on top.

Colombia

An antidote to the ubiquitous sweet and sticky cocktail, this uses the bitterness of the espresso to offset the Kahlua. If you take a spoon of sugar in your coffee, then add the crème de cacao to take the edge off this shot.

INGREDIENTS
Single shot Colombia espresso
35 ml vodka
35 ml Kahlua (coffee liqueur)
25 ml crème de cacao (optional)

GLASS
Large shot glass

STEPS
1 - Combine all the ingredients into a cocktail shaker and shake well.

2 - Strain and pour over shaved ice into a large shot glass.

TIPS FROM THE BAR
This is a great pre-dinner cocktail, but equally, a pick me up later in the evening if you are starting to flag!

The Fred Flintstone

Prior to making this cocktail, make sure you are dressed in the appropriate attire – this should consist of a shredded sleeveless shirt, no socks or underpants and if at all possible, a neckerchief – preferably in a burnt orange.

INGREDIENTS
Triple shot of Kahlua (coffee liqueur)
Single shot of espresso
Dash of Cointreau
Crushed ice

GLASS
Highball glass

GARNISH
Clover leaf

STEPS
1 - Pour ingredients unceremoniously into a cocktail shaker.

2 - Add one scoop of vanilla ice cream.

3 - Next, take your club (or cooking mallet) and smash a handful of ice into small pieces and pour crushed ice into cocktail shaker and shake vociferously for 15 to 20 seconds while at the same time shouting 'Yabba dabba doo'.

4 - Pour into glass and garnish with a clover leaf.

TIPS FROM THE BAR
Tools - In order to make this cocktail, you will require a club; however in this instance a cooking mallet will suffice. A lot of pounding will be needed.

The Black Russian

A popular and worldwide know cocktail, created in 1939 in honour of the U.S. ambassador Perle Mesta. The Black Russian is a simple vodka and coffee liqueur drink. This, and its sister cocktail The White Russian, are said to be one of the first that every cocktail maker should memorise. Traditionally made in two different ways based on its part vodka to coffee liqueur ratio, this 'on the rocks' cocktail is suitable for any palette and a sure way to survive a Moscow winter.

INGREDIENTS

50 ml vodka
25 ml coffee liqueur
Ice cubes
Cola (optional)

GLASS

Rocks Glass

GARNISH

A couple of straws

STEPS

1 - Fill the rocks glass with ice cubes.

2 - Pour vodka over the ice cubes.

3 - Add coffee liqueur into glass.

4 - Top with Cola as desired (optional).

5 - Add a couple of straws to complete your Black Russian.

TIPS FROM THE BAR

To diversify the taste of this classic, why not try experimenting beyond the common coffee liqueurs like Kahlua to create different tastes?

Slippery Nipple

This versatile little drink is at home on the ski slopes as a shot or at the end of a sumptuous dinner party. It is quick and easy to serve and I defy you not to like it.

INGREDIENTS
1 measure Bailey's Irish Cream
1 measure sambuca

GLASS
Shot glass

STEPS
1 - Pour the sambuca into a shot glass.

2 - Float the Bailey's on top. Simple!

Barry White's Sexual Chocolate

This cocktail was created and named by my brother whilst we were experimenting with different mixtures and flavours one drunken evening. It is a milk and cream based cocktail, so perhaps not to everyone's liking but delicious nonetheless.

INGREDIENTS
50 ml Baileys Irish Cream
25 ml Jack Daniels Bourbon
50 ml fresh cream or milk
Crushed ice

GLASS
Tom Collins or water glass

GARNISH
Chocolate sprinkles

STEPS
1 - Pour the baileys and Jack Daniels into the cocktail shaker.

2 - Top up with the milk or cream.

3 - Add the crushed ice and shake vigorously until a layer of condensation forms on the cocktail shaker.

4 - Pour the mixture into the glass.

5 - Top with chocolate sprinkles and enjoy!

Fruit Liqueurs

Sex on the Beach

This cocktail is so smooth and relaxing it should have been named 'better than sex on the beach'! After a hard day in the sun on your holiday on some distant shore what better way to prepare for your evening out than to relax in your favourite beach bar and have the bartender fix you his favourite take on the cocktail. I have come across many variations of the famous drink but my best is at my favourite bar on Waikiki Beach, Hawaii. Here I like to kick back, relax and have a couple of drinks before I find a place to dance. Here's the recipe I copied down last time I visited the bar.

INGREDIENTS
Three-quarters measure of peach schnapps
Three-quarters measure of melon liqueur
Three-quarters measure of Malibu
1 measure of pineapple juice
1 measure of orange juice
1 measure of cranberry juice

GLASS
Large glass

STEPS
1 - Throw everything into a shaker with crushed ice.

2 - Shake vigorously.

3 - Pour into a large glass with some ice.

TIPS FROM THE BAR
If you would like it a bit creamier a blob of cream into the mixer would work a treat, enjoy!

Pink Squirrel

The pink squirrel is a sweet and creamy cocktail well balanced with the almond-like taste of crème de noyauz, a liqueur made from apricot kernels. The pink squirrel is thought to have been invented at Bryant's Cocktail Lounge in Milwaukee by Bryant Sharp. The original recipe had ice cream rather than cream so was rather like a milk shake.

INGREDIENTS
100 ml crème de noyaux
100 ml crème de cacao
30 ml fresh cream

GLASS
Chilled cocktail glass

STEPS
1 - Pour the ingredients into a cocktail shaker filled with ice.

2 - Shake well.

3 - Serve strained into a chilled cocktail glass.

TIPS FROM THE BAR
Many variants of this cocktail substitute the crème de noyauz, (which is often hard to find), with grenadine. Such variants lack the almond flavour and pink colour that defines the pink squirrel.

Skittle Bomb

The skittle bomb is a very simple and easy drink to make, which has become popular amongst night-clubbers because of it tastes similar to Skittles (the children's sweets). The bomb part of the name is derived from dropping the shot glass into another drink. Not the most sophisticated of drinks but this drink will definitely get your weekend started on a Friday night!

INGREDIENTS
45 ml Cointreau
Half a can of Red Bull

GLASS
Shot glass
Highball glass

STEPS
1 - Fill a shot glass with Cointreau.

2 - Simply drop the shot glass into a highball glass with the Red Bull.

3 - Add a splash of fruit cordial if required.

TIPS FROM THE BAR
Fruit-flavoured cordials can also be added to further enhance the taste.

The Fuzzy Navel

The fuzzy navel is lighter on the alcohol and simple to mix, making a great summertime cocktail.

INGREDIENTS
1 or 2 shots (25 ml per shot) peach schnapps
Orange juice to fill
Ice

GLASS

Highball glass

GARNISH

Orange wedge

STEPS

1 - Pour peach schnapps to taste, 1 or 2 shots, into glass over 4 ice cubes.

2 - Fill glass with orange juice and stir well.

3 - Garnish with an orange wedge.

Jagerbomb

The jagerbomb is a bomb shot cocktail that was originally mixed by dropping a shot of Jagermeister liquor into a glass of beer or, more recently, into a glass of Red Bull or other energy drink. Many variations have ensued including a turbo jagerbomb which includes an additional shot of Vodka or an atomic jagerbomb where Red Bull is substituted with Sparks energy drink. A lad bomb is a classic jagerbomb but with a double shot of vodka. This drink is alcoholic and potent hence it should be consumed with caution.

INGREDIENTS
Half a can of Red Bull
1 measure Jagermeister

GLASS
Tumbler glass
Shot glass

STEPS
1 - Empty half a can of Red Bull into tumbler glass.

2 - Drop shot glass of Jagermeister into tumbler.

3 - Drink in one!

TIPS FROM THE BAR
A Lad bomb is a classic jagerbomb but with a double shot of Vodka.

Flaming Sambuca

Sambuca is made from elderberries and is believed to have originated in Arabia as a drink called Zammut. Sambuca became very popular in post WWII Italy, where drinkers would use it to sweeten their coffee instead of sugar. When drinking it neat, it is customary to garnish the drink with the three coffee beans to toast health, happiness and prosperity.

INGREDIENTS
25 ml sambuca
5 drops Blue Curaçao

GLASS
Shot glass

GARNISH
Three coffee beans

STEPS
1 - Pour the sambuca into shot glass.

2 - Add the curacao.

3 - Place a beer mat over the glass and allow fumes to gather before removing and lighting the sambuca.

4 - Once alight, leave it for 10 seconds (no more) then quickly extinguish by placing a beer mat over the glass.

5 - Drink the shot, preferably in one go.

TIPS FROM THE BAR
Do not leave the sambuca flaming for too long before extinguishing as this is likely to result in burning either to the hand or mouth. The vapours are strong and can attach to skin or clothing so care should be taken if your lighting subsequent shots to reduce any risk of fire.

Smoothies
and Mocktails

Banana Strawberry Smoothie

A healthy, nutritious smoothie which is great for breakfast or as a healthy snack in the day. An instant hit with the kids! They also love helping to make this one as it's so easy to make and so yummy. It is also healthy with all the strawberries, banana and yoghurt.

INGREDIENTS

500 grams strawberries, ends removed and sliced
2 ripe bananas, chopped
2-3 scoops of vanilla ice-cream
2 tablespoons honey
120 ml yoghurt
120 ml milk
2-3 scoops ice-cream

GLASS

Tall glass

STEPS

1 - Chill glasses in fridge first.

2 - Place ingredients in a blender and blend until smooth.

3 - Pour into glasses and serve immediately.

TIPS FROM THE BAR

If too thick add more milk. If too thin add more ice cream.

Berry Thrice Smoothie

This smoothie is great for those mornings when your brain is still thinking of bed but your body is headed to work. With all those berries providing you with energy, you'll be set to take on the day. Awaken your taste buds with this healthy fruit smoothie packed full of goodness

INGREDIENTS

500 ml cold skimmed milk
6 strawberries chopped
12 raspberries
18 blueberries
1 tablespoon goji berries
1 tablespoon oats soaked in skimmed milk or apple juice overnight
Crushed ice as required

GLASS

Tall glass

STEPS

1 - Pour milk in a blender and add the strawberries, raspberries, blueberries, goji berries and oats.

2 - Add crushed ice for a colder drink.

3 - Blend on highest speed for 2 minutes or until mixture blended into a smoothie.

Breakfast in a Glass

Looking for an easy breakfast in a glass recipe using health ingredients to kick start your day? Look no further. Very quick and easy to make especially with the hectic busy schedules most people now have, this can be made ahead of time for a grab and go kind of morning. It is the perfect way to start your day, with this breakfast smoothie that will keep you smiling all day.

INGREDIENTS

1 banana
Third cup of orange juice
Half glass of crushed Ice
100 g plain natural yoghurt
1 tablespoon of honey
Quarter teaspoon of ground nutmeg
3 dates (or prunes)
Cocoa powder

GLASS

Collins Glass

STEPS

1 - Chop Banana into quarters.

2 - Drop banana, dates, honey, nutmeg and yoghurt into blender

3 - Blend until smooth.

4 - While blades whirring add orange juice and crushed ice until consistency is as you like it.

5 - Pour into glass.

6 - Garnish with a gentle sprinkle of cocoa powder.

TIPS FROM THE BAR

Adding a dash of cocoa powder will make this smoothie extra special.

Cinderella Fruit Cocktail

Try this refreshing mocktail which brings the refreshing taste of tropical fruit to life.

INGREDIENTS

30 ml lemon juice
30 ml orange juice
30 ml pineapple juice
60 ml ginger ale
Dash of grenadine

GLASS

Tumbler

GARNISH

Pineapple and orange slices

STEPS

1 - Pour the juices into a cocktail shaker with ice cubes.

2 - Shake well.

3 - Strain into a chilled tumbler filled with ice to serve one; or into two cocktail glasses to serve two.

4 - Garnish with the slices of pineapple and/or orange.

TIPS FROM THE BAR

Some people prefer using apple juice or coke as delicious alternatives to pineapple juice.

Chocolate Strawberry Milkshake Smoothie

A special treat! For you or for the one you love. This tastes so good, you will love it. You may feel it's a little naughty but it does contain lots of nutritious value too with all the healthy strawberries and yoghurt. This is a very enjoyable milkshake and is guaranteed to make you smile.

INGREDIENTS

120 ml milk
3 to 4 scoops of vanilla ice cream

GLASS

Long glass

GARNISH

480 ml of fresh strawberries, cut up
1 to 2 tablespoons of chocolate syrup

STEPS

1 - Place all the ingredients in a blender and blend until smooth.

2 - Serve in a long glass.

3 - Garnish with the chocolate syrup and serve with strawberries on the side.

TIPS FROM THE BAR

If too thick then add more milk until the correct consistency is reached.

Fruits and Nuts Smoothie

Apart from the natural benefits of almonds they help provide a little texture to the smoothie.

INGREDIENTS

500 ml cold skimmed milk
1 banana chopped
4 strawberries chopped
Half an avocado, stoned and sliced
1 tablespoon goji berries
2 tablespoons oats soaked in skimmed milk or apple juice overnight
1 tablespoon chopped or sliced almonds
Crushed ice as required

GLASS

Tall glass

STEPS

1 - Pour the milk into a blender.

2 - Add banana, strawberries, avocado, goji berries and oats.

3 - Blend on highest speed for 2 minutes or until mixture blended into a smoothie.

4 - Add almonds and blend for another 20 to 30 seconds.

5 - Pour into the glass and serve.

TIPS FROM THE BAR

Adjust blend time for the almonds to suit your texture preference. Add crushed ice for a colder drink.

Kiwi Strawberry Smoothie

The increased focus on healthier living means a smoothie is a simple and excellent way to consume several of the recommended 5-a-day. Kiwi fruit is a great source of vitamins C and K. Strawberries are also a good source of vitamin C. Both fruits also contain flavonoids which are reported to be anti-carcinogenic. This smoothie is a wonderfully refreshing way to start the day, vitalising the senses, kick-starting the metabolism and putting a spring in the step.

INGREDIENTS
1 medium sized kiwi fruit
10 medium sized strawberries
1 banana
75 ml apple juice

GLASS
Tumbler

STEPS
1 - Peel the kiwi fruit and cut in half.

2 - Husk the strawberries.

3 - Peel the banana, cut away any blemishes and chop into pieces.

4 - Put the fruit together into a blender.

5 - Add ice, around 4 cubes.

6 - Add the apple juice.

7 - Pulse until thoroughly blended and no lumps remain (approx 30-45 seconds).

8 - Pour into a tumbler or other glass.

Lime Mango Smoothie

This has coconut water to keep you hydrated as well as a pinch of cayenne to rev up your metabolism. Yum!

INGREDIENTS
480 ml ripe mango chunks
2 to 3 tablespoons fresh lime juice
480 ml unsweetened coconut water
Pinch of cayenne powder

GLASS

Tall glass

STEPS

1 - Add all ingredients to a blender.

2 - Blend until smooth.

TIPS FROM THE BAR

Some prefer to replace coconut water and cayenne with 1 tray of ice cubes and 2 table spoons of icing sugar a delicious and refreshing summer drink. Add rum to make an excellent cocktail.

Mango Lassi Smoothie

Lassi is the drink which originated in the Punjab, India. It is now, however, popular around the world. Lassi is yoghurt based and traditionally is a savoury drink and can be flavoured with spices such as cumin and cardamons. Mango lassi is a sweeter refreshing drink, drunk in the summer months, usually drunk in the afternoons or after dinner.

INGREDIENTS
240 ml peeled, chopped and cubed mango
240 ml low fat plain yoghurt
I tablespoon sugar
120 ml of milk
Quarter teaspoon of vanilla
Pinch of salt
Quarter teaspoon of cardamom

GLASS
Tall glass

STEPS
1 - Place all the ingredients in a blender and blend until smooth.

2 - Serve immediately in a tall glass.

3 - Add ice if desired.

Mango Pineapple Smoothie

This flavoursome smoothie has all the flavours of a tropical paradise. Be transported to a white sandy beach and tropical music playing in your ears! It is a great way to start your day, a healthy, filling drink which also gets your taste buds buzzing. The yoghurt in the drink provides you with protein too. The drink can be consumed anytime, if the weather's good or if you have leftover fruit ingredients and is easy to make. Have fun mixing the smoothie and imagine sipping it on a tropical beach!

INGREDIENTS
240 ml chopped fresh pineapple
One and a half mangoes, peeled and cubed
240 ml vanilla yoghurt
120 ml milk
3 or 4 ice cubes

GLASS

Tall glass

STEPS

1 - Place all the ingredients in a blender and blend until smooth.

2 - Serve in a tall glass and enjoy.

TIPS FROM THE BAR

If the smoothie is too thick add more milk. If the smoothie is too thin add more ice.

Mint and Rosemary Ice Tea Thirst Quencher

A classic fruit tea that is made from ingredients that can be grown in gardens, window boxes or, failing this, found in the supermarket. Particularly good for a hot summer afternoon, this can also be made with hot water for a winter warmer drink.

INGREDIENTS

1 litre boiled water
3 sprigs fresh mint (about 20 leaves) de-stalked and chopped (easier using scissors)
Half a sprig of rosemary de-stalked and chopped (easier using scissors)
Honey for sweetness if required

GLASS

Tall glass

STEPS

1 - Pour the boiling water into a large stainless steel teapot (or one that can be heated on the hob).

2 - Add the chopped mint and rosemary.

3 - Heat the teapot gently for no more than on 1 or 2 minutes.

4 - Remove the teapot off the hob add the lemon and leave to cool.

5 - Once cool pour contents over a sieve onto a water jug or similar container.

6 - Transfer the lemon from the sieve to the water jug and place in fridge to cool. Add some honey if required for sweetness.

Strawberry Milkshake

Thick, creamy and indulgent. The oldest known reference to the milkshake dates back to 1885. In this, one of the ingredients was whiskey, apparently for medicinal purposes only.

INGREDIENTS
250 grams fresh strawberries washed and sliced
3 tablespoons white sugar
480 ml whole milk
550 ml of strawberry ice cream
250 grams smooth strawberry yoghurt

GLASS
Tall chilled glasses

GARNISH
Two large fresh strawberries

STEPS
1 - Place the sliced strawberries into a bowl, sprinkle with sugar and place in the freezer for one hour.

2 - Once frozen blend the strawberries with the milk and yoghurt until smooth. No chunks please!

3 - Begin to add the ice cream to the blender, large spoonfuls at a time. Blend, then add some more and so on until the mixture is thoroughly blended.

4 - Pour the mixture into a chilled glass.

5 - Garnish with a strawberry and enjoy.

TIPS FROM THE BAR
Make it more healthy by swapping the yoghurt for a low fat option and use skimmed milk instead of whole. Do not use sugar to sweeten your strawberries and remove the ice cream from the recipe

Virgin Mojito

The mojito is one of the most famous rum-based highballs originating from the island of Cuba. The traditional Cuban recipe uses spearmint of yerba buena which are very popular on the island. The virgin mojito is a sweet, tangy cocktail which has become very popular in restaurants and cocktail bars.

When out partying it is a great alternative to the usual soft drink for non-drinkers, which only contains about 145 calories, as long as you stick to the traditional version avoiding the pre-packaged, syrupy mix.

INGREDIENTS

8 sprigs of mint
2 fresh lime.
1 teaspoon of brown sugar
Half a glass of Soda Water
Quarter of a glass of apple juice
1 glass of crushed ice

GLASS

Highball glass

GARNISH

Lime Wedge
Fresh sugar cane

STEPS

1 - Break mint leaves with hands. For more flavour, break them into small pieces.

2 - Chop half a lime into slices.

3 - Drop the chopped mint leaves, lime slices and a teaspoon of sugar to the highball glass.

4 - Muddle the mint, lime and brown sugar using a muddler or a fork mixing everything together to bring out the flavour of mints and lime.

5 - Using half a lime squeeze fresh lime into the glass.

6 - Add crushed ice.

7 - Add the soda water and the apple juice

8 - Garnish with a slice of lime on the side of the glass and stick of fresh sugar cane added to the drink.

9 - Gently stir, serve with a straw and enjoy.

Virgin Strawberry Daiquiri

This is a modern version of a classic Spanish cocktail that includes rum, citrus (typically lime juice) and sugar. Although the alcoholic version of this cocktail is delicious, it's also quite straightforward to make a non-alcoholic version that is perfect for people who don't like drinking, can't drink, are not of legal drinking age.

This is a wonderful refreshing drink, perfect for a hot summer's day which is great for garden parties or barbecues. The strawberries are tangy and thirst-quenching. As its fruit flavoured and blended, you're less likely to notice the missing alcohol. If you have the option I'd suggest fresh strawberries over frozen; the flavour will be much better.

INGREDIENTS

12 fresh strawberries, red, ripe and without the tops (can use frozen if strawberries are out of season).
30 ml fresh lime juice.
Quarter teaspoon pure vanilla extract
1 teaspoon of sugar
150 ml (or half glass) lemonade
1 glass of crushed ice

GLASS

Highball glass

GARNISH

Orange wedge

STEPS

1 - Fill a blender with strawberries, lime juice, vanilla extract, sugar and lemonade.

2 - Blend until smooth.

3 - Take one highball glass, fill with crushed ice.

4 - Add cracked ice to the blender and blend again until smooth.

5 - Pour into a chilled cocktail glass.

6 - Garnish with an orange slice on the side of the glass.

TIPS FROM THE BAR

For fun, you can always add a straw, cocktail umbrella or other decorations.

Index of Main Cocktail Ingredients

Index of Cocktail Names

Index of Smoothie and Mocktail Names

www.ingramcontent.com/pod-product-compliance
Lightning Source LLC
LaVergne TN
LVHW021508080426
835509LV00018B/2435